Let's Joke Around!

LET'S TELL JOKES ABOUT DOGS

Leonard Clasky

WINDMILL BOOKS

Published in 2023 by Windmill Books, an Imprint of Rosen Publishing
2544 Clinton St., Buffalo, NY 14224

Disclaimer: Portions of this work were originally authored by Maria Nelson and published as *Jokes and More About Dogs*. All new material this edition authored by Leonard Clasky.

Editor: Caitie McAneney
Book Design: Rachel Rising

Photo Credits: Cover Chutima Chaochaiya/Shutterstock.com; cover, p. 1, pp. 3-24 (background) V_ctoria/Shutterstock.com; p. 4 Jagodka/Shutterstock.com; p. 5 Erik Lam/Shutterstock.com; pp. 6, 8, 10, 12, 14, 16, 18, 20, 22 VectorShow/Shutterstock.com; p. 7 Africa Studio/Shutterstock.com; p. 9 dezy/Shutterstock.com; p. 11 Lim Tiaw Leong/Shutterstock.com; p. 13 Anna Goroshnikova/Shutterstock.com; p. 15 Jucadima/Shutterstock.com; p. 17 WilleeCole Photography/Shutterstock.com; p. 19 Andrea Izzotti/Shutterstock.com; p. 21 Tara Lynn and Co/Shutterstock.com.

Cataloging-in-Publication Data
Names:Clasky, Leonard.
Title: Let's tell jokes about dogs / Leonard Clasky.
Description: New York : Windmill Books, 2023. | Series: Lets's Joke Around!| Includes glossary.
Identifiers: ISBN 9781538392850 (pbk.) | ISBN 9781538392867 (library bound) | ISBN 9781538392874 (ebook)
Subjects: LCSH: Dogs, humor -Juvenile literature. | Jokes -Juvenile literature.
Classification: LCC PN6231.D68 C53 2023 | DDC 818/.602-dc23

Manufactured in the United States of America

CPSIA Compliance Information: Batch #CWWM23. For further information contact Rosen Publishing at 1-800-237-9932.

CONTENTS

MOST POPULAR PET

Descended from wild wolves, dogs are now the most popular pet in the world. They've earned the nickname "man's best friend." In fact, almost half of U.S. dogs sleep in their owner's bed!

It's no wonder people love dogs so much. Many dogs love to cuddle, play, and learn tricks. They have amazing **senses** of smell and hearing. Each dog has a special nose print, just like we have fingerprints. Let's learn some jokes that are as silly as a puppy chasing its tail!

THERE ARE HUNDREDS OF DOG **BREEDS**, FROM HUGE GREAT DANES TO TINY CHIHUAHUAS.

DOG FOOD!

WHAT DOES A DOG CHEF SAY?

"Bone-appétit!"

WHAT DO DOGS EAT AT THE MOVIES?

Pupcorn.

WHAT DO DOGS LIKE TO EAT FOR DESSERT?

Pupcakes.

WHAT DO DALMATIANS SAY AFTER A GOOD DINNER?
"That hit the spots!"

DOGS IN SUMMER

WHY WAS THE DOG SWEATING SO MUCH?
It was a hot dog!

WHERE DO DOGS CAMP IN THE SUMMER?
A pup tent!

WHAT DO YOU GIVE A DOG WITH A FEVER?
Ketchup—it's the best thing for a hot dog!

WHAT DO YOU CALL A SHEEPDOG IN A GARDEN?
A collie-flower!

DOGS IN WINTER

WHY DID THE DOG WEAR A SWEATER?
He was a chili dog!

WHAT DO YOU CALL A DOG WHO PLAYS IN THE SNOW?
A slush puppy!

WHAT DO YOU CALL A DOG THAT'S BEEN OUT IN THE COLD?
A pupsicle!

WHY SHOULD YOU WATCH WHERE YOU WALK WHEN IT'S RAINING CATS AND DOGS?
You might step in a poodle!

DOGS ON THE MOVE!

WHAT GENRE OF MUSIC DO DOGS DANCE TO?

Pup music.

WHY AREN'T DOGS GOOD DANCERS?

They have two left feet!

WHERE SHOULD YOU NEVER TAKE A DOG?

A flea market.

WHAT DO YOU CALL A DOG THAT PRACTICES YOGA?
A foldin' retriever!

DIFFERENT DOGS

WHAT DO YOU CALL A CANINE MAGICIAN?
A Labra-cadabra-dor.

WHAT DO YOU CALL A DOG THAT CAN'T STOP SNEEZING?
A-choo-wawa!

WHAT KIND OF DOG DOESN'T LIKE TO THROW THINGS AWAY?
A **hoarder** collie.

WHAT'S A WITCH'S FAVORITE DOG?
A Yorkshire scarier.

DOG WORDPLAY

HOW DO FLEAS TRAVEL ON DOGS?

By itch-hiking.

WHAT'S A DOG'S FAVORITE PIZZA TOPPING?

Pupperoni!

WHAT DO **MARINE BIOLOGISTS** AND DOGS HAVE IN COMMON?

One tags a whale, and the other wags a tail!

WHY DID THE TWO DOGS GET MARRIED?

They caught the love pug.

BEST BARK

WHERE DO DOGS PARK THEIR CARS?
In the barking lot.

WHAT DO DOGS AND TREES HAVE IN COMMON?
They both have bark.

WHAT DO YOU TELL A YOUNG DOG WHO WON'T STOP BARKING?
"Hush, puppy!"

WHAT DO YOU GET WHEN YOU MIX A DOG AND A FROG?
A croaker spaniel!

DOGGIE TROUBLE!

WHAT DID THE DOG TELL THE FLEA?

"Stop bugging me!"

WHAT DID THE COWBOY SAY WHEN HIS DOG RAN OFF?

"Well, doggone!"

WHAT SHOULD YOU DO IF YOUR DOG TRIES TO EAT YOUR DICTIONARY?

Take the words out of his mouth!

WHAT DID THE DOG NEED AFTER HE ROLLED AROUND IN MUD?
Some sham-poodle!

FUN DOG FACTS!

- Dogs have dreams! Older dogs and puppies dream the most often.
- Many people have called the basenji a "barkless" dog. It might not bark like a normal dog, but it can **yodel**!
- The United States has more pet dogs than any other country in the world.
- The longest dog tongue ever belonged to a boxer named Brandy. It was 17 inches (43 cm) long!
- Dogs are about as smart as a two-year-old human. Border collies are the smartest breed.

GLOSSARY

breed: A group of animals that share features different from other groups of their kind.

descended: Born of a certain group or family.

genre: A certain type, sort, or category.

hoarder: Someone who collects or saves up many things.

marine biologist: A scientist who studies living things in the water.

sense: Any of five ways to understand or experience one's surroundings.

yodel: To make a sound by changing from a natural voice to one much higher in pitch, and quickly back again.

FOR MORE INFORMATION

Books

Fitzgerald, Stephanie. *A Pack of Dogs.* New York, NY: Children's Press, 2023.

Jeffries, Corina. *We Can Draw Dogs.* New York, NY: Windmill Books, 2023.

Lynch, Seth. *Dogs Close Up.* New York, NY: Gareth Stevens Publishing, 2023.

Websites

11 Funny Animal Jokes for Kids (and Kids at Heart)
nationalzoo.si.edu/animals/news/11-funny-animal-jokes-for-kids-and-kids-heart
Check out more funny animal jokes to share with your friends.

10 Awesome Dog Facts!
www.natgeokids.com/uk/discover/animals/general-animals/dog-facts/
Learn more fun facts about dogs with *National Geographic Kids*!